THE CHANGING

Marston

BOOK ONE

Carole Newbigging
and
Angela Wood

Robert Boyd
PUBLICATIONS

3-00

CW00525006

Published by
Robert Boyd Publications
260 Colwell Drive
Witney, Oxfordshire OX8 7LW

First published 1996

ISBN 1 899536 07 8

OTHER TITLES IN THE
CHANGING FACES SERIES
Cowley
Cowley: Book Two
Summertown and Cutteslowe
Botley and North Hinksey
Headington: Book One
Littlemore and Sandford
Woodstock
Marston: Book One
Cumnor and Farmoor with Appleton and Eaton

Printed and bound in Great Britain at The Alden Press, Oxford

Contents

Acknowledgements   4

Preface   4

Foreword   5

Introduction   5

Map of Old Marston 1937   8

Section   1 St Nicholas Church   9

Section   2 Around Old Marston   19

Section   3 Mill Lane Area   43

Section   4 The Ferry   53

Section   5 School and Recreation   57

Section   6 New Marston   69

Area map of Old and New Marston 1922   79

Cover illustrations

Front: Marston Post Office c1890.

Back: William Street, New Marston, early this century.

Acknowledgements

The success of any book depends on its content, particularly in a photographic book of this type, commemorating the changes that have taken place within a district, and the people and families who have contributed to its development.

The compilers gratefully acknowledge the help and assistance given so willingly by so many people. In particular they thank the following for permission to use personal photographs, and for assistance given in identifying those photographs: Mrs V Andrews, Mrs G Batts, Mr J Bleay, Mr and Mrs H Bridges, Miss H Clifford, Mrs B Deam, Mr H Deam, Mr H Elmey, Mr A Gammon, Mrs L Harley, Mrs E Hewlett, Mr G Hughes, Mrs L Hughes, Mr A Jones, Mrs B King, Mrs K Lewis, Mrs G Penny, Rev T Price, Mrs T Prickett, Mr A Rhymes, Mr and Mrs Rickets, Mr J Smith, Rev P Rimmer, Mrs A Spokes Symonds, Miss W Tomlinson, Mr G Ward, Mr L Walters, Mr D Woodward, also members of the British Legion and the Women's Institute, the landlords of The White Hart and The Bricklayers, and Govenors of St Nicholas and St Michael's Schools. In addition we acknowledge assistance given by the Photographic Archives of the Centre for Oxfordshire Studies, Reed Information Services, the Bodleian Library and the Ashmolean Museum.

Special thanks to Chris Fenn for the map, and to the Marston Women's Institute for permission to quote from their notebook, both of which we believe enhance the readers enjoyment and appreciation of the area.

Preface

During the course of preparation, so much photographic history was uncovered that it was decided that two books should result. How then to separate the content? Whilst recognising the very different characters of Old and New Marston, they are inextricably entwined in their development. Book 1 covers, in the main, the original part of Marston, with its thatched cottages, ponds, and manor house, but also includes the early New Marston development of William Street and Ferry and Edgeware Roads, with New Marston School and St Nicholas Chapel of Ease in Ferry Road. In some instances photographs of a later period have been included where it was thought appropriate.

Book 2, to be published during 1997, will continue the development and activities of the Marston district as a whole. Material is still being collected and we would be delighted to hear from anyone with memories and, more particularly, photographs of this area.

Foreword

I remember the apples laid in rows on the polished wooden floor of the long lounge of the Harlow's home, opposite The Three Horshoes pub in Marston. Professor Vincent Harlow, librarian of Rhodes House at that time, and Gretta, his wife, had joined together two thatched cottages to form one house. The year was 1935, the year of the Silver Jubilee of King George V and Queen Mary. My parents were looking up my brothers, then studying at Oxford, and decided, whilst there, to look up the Harlows, who were old friends of the family.

Little could I have dreamt at that time that Vincent Harlow, who was a favourite visitor to our home when I was a youngster, would, in years to come, visit Joan, my wife, and myself in our home in the Nilgiri Hills in South India. Little did he or I conceive that, out of the blue, the Bishop of Oxford would write to him, as churchwarden of St Nicholas Church, Marston, and request him to interview me as a possible incumbent for the parish! (At my interview with Vincent, and his fellow churchwarden, Bernard Oliver, he didn't let on that he'd known me since the age of four!) Sadly Vincent died early on in my incumbency. Not only was he wise and supportive, but many will remember how he joined in the entertainment at parish parties, once dressed as The Lincolnshire Poacher! The restored gallery in St Nicholas Church commemorates his life and service to Church and Commonwealth. The local school, which later sadly changed its title, was named after him.

In those early days one approached Marston along Elsfield Road, through a cathedral nave of elms. There were a number of caravan sites, often muddy underfoot in wet weather. One caravan I remember well was that of Albert and Zoe King, with the exciting name of 'The Golden Journey'. Albert ran the art shop at the Polytechnic, and in his spare time would often be seen with his watercolours, painting scenes around the village. With his telescope on a starry night he would point out Saturn and her moons to our children. Houses were springing up everywhere, and the name of 'A J Pye, Builders' was on many boards.

The Primary School was filled to capacity, and May Day still had its maypole, with the 'Queen' and her attendants. In those days Clare, my daughter, rang the bell at the Victoria Arms and crossed over to school by ferry. There was no Marston Ferry link road, and many of us, perhaps shortsightedly, opposed the idea at the time.

But Marston was a wonderful parish to serve as its incumbent. I like to think that it maintained, and I trust still maintains, its rebel 'Cromwellian' spirit, challenging outside pressures which might destroy its character and charm.

It was a privilege to be vicar of the parish for 31 years (John Mortimer, one of my predecessors, was incumbent for 46 years). For Joan, my wife, myself and my family, Marston will always be the focus of so many friendships and memories.

It is a privilege also to be invited to write a foreword to this book, which I'm sure will not only fascinate newcomers but evoke many memories amongst others who open its pages.

Paul N Rimmer
October 1996

Introduction

"The town, as it is called, of Marston consists of 43 dwelling houses, the number of inhabitants are about 250. There is no house or habitation in any other part of the parish, except the hut of a solitary fisherman on the bank of the Cherwell, where he resides for the purpose of attending his nets and his wheels. No person above the rank of a yeoman dwells in this parish at present. The family of Croke inhabited the manor house before, during and after the grand rebellion. Another branch of the family also dwelt here. The house of the latter is now an ale-house, distinguished by the sign of the White Hart, in the possession of Mr Joseph Bleay, an old and respectable inhabitant, who carries on the triple employment of a farmer, a baker, and a publican. Luxury has not yet extended to Marston, near as it is to the University and a populous city. The farmers are most of them persons possessed of considerable property, yet they live in the most frugal and plain manner. The names most general here are Sims, Bley, and Loder, and there are several families bearing each name." So stated the February 1800 issue of *The Gentleman's Magazine.*

The village of Marston lies about two miles north east of Oxford on the east side of the River Cherwell, surrounding by low-lying marshy land. This situation has given the village its name deriving from the Anglo-Saxon 'Merstun' or 'Marsh Town'. The first written reference to Marston was thought to be that of 1122, when Henry I granted the chapel of Marston to the canons of St Frideswide's, but an earlier mention was made in 1065 during the time of Edward the Confessor, concerning the kings gift of his estate at Islip and half hide of land at Marston (Mersee) to the monks of Westminster. In 1279 there are records of 46 unfree tenants of the manor of Headington, together with the vicar and two freeholders, one possibly at Court Place, the other the miller, Hugh de Molendino.

It is the Hundred Rolls of 1279 that also give the first mention of a ferry across the River Cherwell, at which time it was held as a freehold by two fishermen. There is, however, no map that locates it until the Ordnance Survey of 1876. It is believed that a temporary bridge existed at Marston during the Civil War to connect the village and north Oxford.

Marston, *'or Ma-son, as the old folks used to call it'* was a tiny hamlet attached to the Manor of Headington. In 1451 the parishes of Headington and Marston were united by a papal bull, and it was not until 1637 that Marston became a separate parish.

Marston was surrounded by forest, where tenants had rights of commoning cattle and cutting furze, fern and dead wood. In 1661 Shotover and Stow Wood were disafforested and the tenants of Marston received 90 acres in compensation, later commuted to a gift of fuel, and eventually of money, known as Forest Coal, dispensed by the church wardens, and only discontinued in the early 1960s.

Colleges with land at Marston included Oriel, Magdalen, Brasenose and Corpus Christi. Brasenose continued to own property until recently, selling Court Place in 1956, and Colthorn Farm (Grange Farm) after the new Marston Ferry Road (completed in 1972) made it no longer viable economically. The college still owns a small piece of land behind Brasenose Cottages.

Several of the old field names are commemorated in modern street and house names, such as Hedley (now Headley), Brookfield, Stockleys, Colthorn, Marsh Lane, Bradlands and Gorse Leas.

Marston village remained a country community for many hundreds of years. During the 19th century development took place south of Marston village, and in 1891 the district of New Marston was separated from the ancient hamlet. On 8 April 1929 New Marston was included in the City of Oxford, due to the extension of the City Boundary which, up to that time, had ended at the lane leading to Kings Mill. On 28 September 1963 New Marston became a separate parish, St Michael and All Angels, with the Rev. Constantine Hope as its first Vicar. At this time the population was around 4000 and still increasing.

On the north, the boundary between Marston and Elsfield follows the course of the Bayswater Brook; the southern boundary runs between the ancient parishes of Headington and Marston from the Kings Mill on the Cherwell to the nearest point on the Oxford–Marston road. The boundary between the county borough and the civil parish of Marston now follows the course of a stream immediately north of New Marston.

The northern by-pass road was not opened until 1932, and the Marston Ferry Link Road, the first road-bridge between Magdalen Bridge and Islip, in 1971. Until then Marston was fairly isolated, and this may have accounted for a noticeable dialect as mentioned in the Gentleman's Magazine of 1800: *There are some peculiar expressions used by the natives of Marston, among which the word 'unked' is most frequently introduced in conversation. Everything that is unfortunate or unlucky, or not as it could be wished, is unked. The word may be derived from 'uncouth', and has in many instances the same meaning. When the roads are miry and dirty it is said to be 'hoxey', and when they are clean and dry, it is 'quite path'.*

Memories of family life in Marston village during the late nineteenth century, as recorded by past members of the Women's Institute, contain many interesting details, for example: *I remember Rasping Pudding, made from the raspings of bread, got from the bakehouse, soaked and boiled in a cloth, and served with honey, sugar or treacle. The poorer people cooked food all in one pot, bacon and potatoes in a net, greens and a suet pudding. The children were given kettle-banger, made by pouring boiling water on the broken bread, served with sugar. Bread of course was always homemade. Hop tops and nettles were cooked as a vegetable. Tea was too expensive being six and eight shillings a pound, the children were given toastwater. Most people kept bees — everything that happened in the family, the bees had to be told by tapping on the hive and giving them the news.*

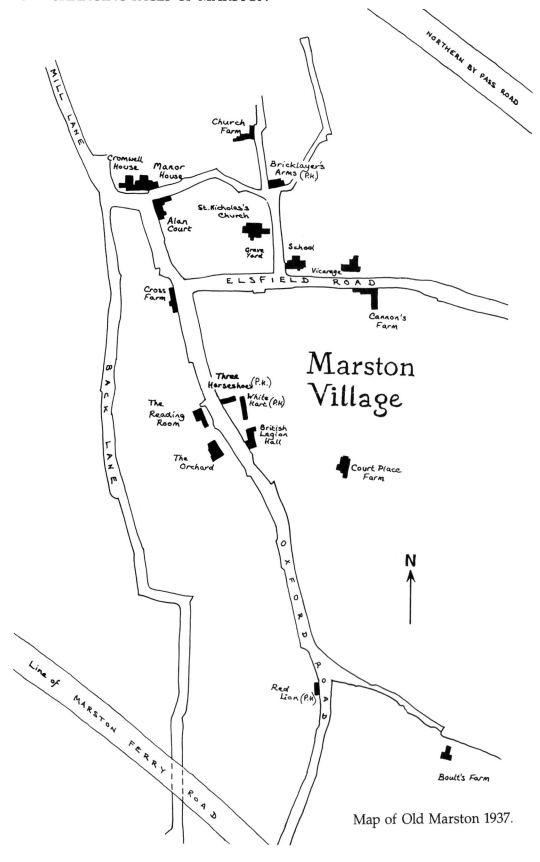

Map of Old Marston 1937.

SECTION ONE

St Nicholas Church

From *Pleasant Spots round Oxford* by Alfred Rimmer.

The church of St Nicholas, dedicated to the patron saint of sea-farers, pawn-brokers, children, and all people in trouble, is first mentioned in 1122, when Henry I granted the chapel of Marston to the canons of St Frideswide's. The chancel arch and seven arches of the nave survive from this period. During the 15th century the aisles were widened and the clerestory, chancel and tower were built. Remnants of wall paintings have been discovered. The Church was endowed with land by the lord of the manor of Headington at the end of the twelfth century. A further endowment for a rood light was made in the fifteenth century by John Chichele, and armorial titles of this period in the chancel indicate a possible connection with Archbishop Chichele. The first major rebuilding of the church took place at this time.

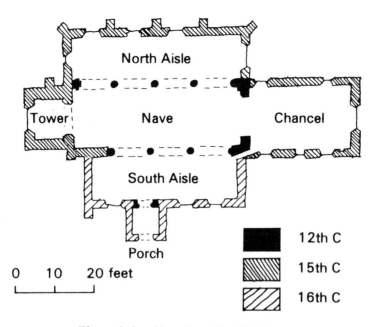

■	12th C
▨	15th C
▱	16th C

0   10   20 feet

Plan of the Church of St Nicholas.

During the reformation the endowment was withdrawn and the connection with St Frideswide's Priory ended. The church and its possessions then became part of the endowment of Cardinal College, later Christ Church. In 1547 the rectory, vicarage and advowson of Marston and Headington were bought by Sir John Brome, lord of the manor of Headington. The rectory estate became merged with that of the manor and it was probably the manor's responsibility to find priests from Oxford colleges to serve the church.

The church from Church Lane, photographed by H W Taunt c1890.

War Memorial

In the churchyard to the left of the entrance gate, a stone cross has been erected, about nine feet high, with an octagonal plinth on two steps. The cross has a quatrefoil motif. On the front of the plinth are the words: 1914 1918 Lest We Forget.

Inside the church on the west wall of the south aisle is a white marble tablet, mounted on mottled black marble, flanked by British Legion flags. The names recorded in Remembrance of the Great War 1914-1918 are:

Maj Reginald D'Arcy Anderson, RGA
Pte Ernest Victor Biovois, Gloucs
Pte Albert John Drewitt, OBLI
Pte Arthur Drewitt, OBLI
LC George Herbert Cummings, OBLI
Pte John Eadle

LC Albert Edward Haynes, R Berks
Pte Herbert George Haynes, RF
Dvr Richard Charles Knibbs, RHA
Cpl Ernest Alfred Ward, OBLI
Pte Henry George Ward, OBLI
Bomr Charles Henry Webb, RGA

Added to the foot of the memorial are the names for World War Two 1939-1945:

Cpl Frederick Gordon Matthews, RMCdo
Sgt Henry Byhette Simms, OBLI
AB Dennis William Ward, RN

St Nicholas Church showing the 1914—18 War Memorial and the lych gate erected in 1927 in memory of H A Cumberlege, a former vicar.

Repairs were carried out in 1956, including strengthening of the tower, renovation of the roof of the chancel and south aisle and restoration of the gargoyle heads at each corner at the top of the tower. This was at the cost of £3,337, most of which was raised by the parish, under the leadership of the Rev Gordon Savage. The lead roof of the nave and north aisle were renewed in 1966.

The East window is over 500 years old, and contains many fragments of old glass. The major proportion of the glass was put in by Miss Rippington in 1903. Other glass in the church commemorates members of the Cannon and Sims families in the 19th century.

The Marston Chalice

This chalice was given to the church by a wealthy Oxford butcher and bailiff, G Skydmore, who died in 1478. The chalice is mounted on three talbot dogs and stands nearly 6 inches tall, and is thought to be the oldest chalice in England.

It is interesting to note that the 1851 census for Marston shows a Henry Skitmore aged 5, grandson of Francis and Amy Cummins, cordwainer, a possible descendent of the original donor of the Marston Chalice.

John Hamilton Mortimer was Vicar of Marston from 1904 to 1951, over 46 years. He is fondly remembered by many as a faithful and devoted parish priest. He was accustomed to play a hymn each night on the bells. This he did without any aid, even in his latest years. The Rev Mortimer was instrumental in establishing a recreation ground for the village, diminished in 1972 by the building of the Marston Ferry Link Road. He also gave his name to Mortimer Hall.

The Rev Gordon Savage, vicar of Marston from 1952 to 1957, and later the Bishop of Southwell.

The Rev Paul Rimmer, vicar of Marston from 1959 to 1990, seen here with Olive Lodge, one of the first women to be made a Deaconess on 1 November 1972. Olive Lodge lived and worked in Marston for 14 years.

Rimmer Close and Lodge Close are named after the Rev Rimmer and Olive Lodge.

The 100th peal of bells was rung on Saturday 23 June 1990 as a farewell compliment to the Rev Paul Rimmer, after 31 years as Vicar of the parish.

The Marston Ringers

The first mention of bells in the church of St Nicholas appears in the churchwarden accounts of 1547. Over the years the bells have rung for many occasions, and the Marston Ringers can boast several world records within the 'ringing' world. In 1932 George Plumley was elected Master of the Belfry. He chose as his team Charles Gurden, A Bleay, A Cummings, Leonard Plumley, John Eadle, Arthur Drewitt, Newland Bennett, Clifford Colley and George Jennings.

Monday 7 April 1958 was a famous day for the Marston bellringers when they rang a peal of Doubles, 12,600 changes in 6 hours and 20 minutes thus creating a world record and beating the record set by Whaplode, Lincolnshire in 1775. This was achieved under the leadership of Alec Gammon, who had joined the Marston Ringers in 1948.

MARSTON, OXFORD.
THE OXFORD DIOCESAN GUILD.
On Mon., April 7, 1958, in 6 Hours and 20 Minutes,
AT THE CHURCH OF ST. NICHOLAS,
A PEAL OF 12600 DOUBLES
Comprising 3,240 of Reverse St. Bartholomew and 3,120 each of Grandsire, Reverse Canterbury Pleasure and Plain Bob Doubles.
Tenor 6 cwt.

DAVID C. WOODWARD	.. *Treble*	MALCOLM JOURNEAUX	.. 3
ALEC GAMMON 2		ROY H. JONES	4
	CLIVE HOLLOWAY	.. .. *Tenor*	

Arranged by ALEC GAMMON.   Conducted by CLIVE HOLLOWAY.
25th peal on the bells. Longest length of Doubles yet rung, exceeding that of 10,080 rung at Whaplode, Lincs, on February 27th, 1775, in 7 hours 26 minutes by 2,520 changes.

The Marston ringers in 1954, taken in the garden of the Old Vicarage. Left to right: Sidney Wilkins, Roy Jones, Sheila Burden, Clive Holloway, Christine Woodward, Reverend Gordon Savage, Kenneth Tasker, Judith Tasker, Alec Gammon, Rosemary Green, David Woodward, William Brain.

Some of the St Nicholas Handbell Ringers in 1961. Left to right: Leonard Porter, Leonard Maund, Miss Williams, Margaret Cozier, David Oliver, Helen Williams, Julia Chandler, Andrew Dunckley, Noel Deam. At this time the bells were played in the streets at Christmas and, by invitation, at Alan Court.

Group of ringers in October 1969. Left to right: Adrian Buck, Roy Jones, Stephen Buck, Martin Bolton, Len Porter. *At Christmas, after ringing at the church, the ringers with handbells used to go to the houses and farms and finish up with a meal, after which they would make with church-warden pipes and ring the old songs.* Memories of an earlier time: Women's Institute Notebook

PC William Brain (1890–1959), a well known character in Marston. PC Brain was a valued member of the Marston Ringers and the choir and served as church verger.

Independent Order of Oddfellows — Manchester Unity. The Marston Lodge was called Duke of Albany. Pictured here opposite the church c1910, being led by the Marston Drum and Fife Band. The man holding the banner on the right hand side is Mark Edwards. Others include Albert Griffin, William Roberts and Arthur 'Peggy' Bleay, so called because of his peg-leg.

by the Rev. John Hamilton Mortimer M.A. of Magdalen College, Oxford. There is a Mission room at New Marston, connected with the church. One hundred acres of land in this parish are let for the benefit of the proprietors of Marston, and of the poor; the portion assigned to the poor is fixed by a committee according to a scale agreed upon; the rent charge is termed "Forest money." A portion of the Forest farm formerly belonged to the poor of Marston, given to them in lieu of forest rights in the time of Charles II.; this has been sold and is now vested in the Charity Commissioners; the income is distributed yearly in coal. The village cross, distinct from that formerly on the road at a point now marked by a cross cut in the wall by the roadside, it was taken down about 1830 on the alleged reason that it impeded the traffic, and the materials used for mending the road and making some granary stairs in the village. The old manor house, the residence during the Civil War of Unton Croke esq. was for the most part removed in 1843 and partly replaced by stone cottages; the portion of the old house still remaining retains on the north side two gable windows and a blocked doorway, and is called "Cromwell Castle": here in 1645 (May 22), Cromwell and Fairfax met to take measures for the siege of Oxford, and the mansion was also used as a place of meeting in May, 1646, by the Royal and Parliamentary Commissioners during the negotiations for the surrender of the city. To the Croke family, of Marston, belonged the eccentric wanderer, Charles Croke, who, in 1667, under the pseudonym of "Rodolphus," published an account of his rambles, entitled "Youth's Inconstancy." The Colonel Hoole is lord of the manor. The principal landowners are Brasenose and Corpus Christi colleges, the University of Oxford and the trustees of the late Edwin Rippington esq. The soil is loam and clay; subsoil, clay and gravel. The land is chiefly pasture, but wheat and barley are also grown. The area is 1,160 acres; rateable value, £4,120; the population in 1911 was 716. Part of New Marston is in the parish of Headington.

Parish Clerk, Richard Ward.

Post Office.—Richard Joseph Ward, sub-postmaster. Letters arrive through Oxford at 6.45 a.m. & 1.20 p.m. & dispatched at 3.10 & 5.55 p.m. week days; on sundays 11.30 p.m. Headington is the nearest money order & telegraph office. Postal orders are issued here, & paid

Post Office, New Marston.—Mrs. Louisa Carter, sub-postmistress. Letters arrive through Oxford at 7.15 a.m. & 1.15 p.m.; sundays, 7.15 a.m.; dispatched at 7.40 a.m. & 3 & 6.10 p.m.; sundays, 11.40 p.m. St. Clement's is the nearest money order & telegraph office. Postal orders are issued here, & paid

PARISH COUNCIL.
(Consisting of 7 members.)
Chairman, George Evans
Messrs. C. Webb, Arthur Evans, George Evans, R. J. Ward, S. G. Buckett, John Badlo & William Roberts
Clerk, J. W. H. Brown
National School (mixed), erected in 1851, enlarged in 1887 & 1894; it will now hold 125 children; average attendance, 78; Hubert William John Pugh, master
CARRIERS.—Willis, to Oxford, daily, except thurs.; Sumner & Poulton, wed. & sat

Marston.

PRIVATE RESIDENTS.

Brown J. W. H. Almonds farm
Cannon Miss, Fernbank
Cave Miss, Manor house
Gordon Miss, Little Acreage
Honour John, The Orchard
Killmaster Arthur, Bolts lodge
Lamburn Richard
Martin Miss, The Lodge
Mortimer Rev. John Hamilton M.A. [vicar], The Vicarage
Pugh Hubert William John, Rose villa
Rippington Mrs. E. The Elms

COMMERCIAL.

Bleny Walter, carter
Broughton Henry W. farmer, Court Place farm
Brown John Wilfred Hugh, clerk to Parish Council & assistant overseer, Almonds farm
Cotmore Charles F. beer retailer
Cross George, dairy farmer
Drewett Mrs. shopkeeper
Evans Arthur, White Hart P.H
Haynes Charles Henry, farmer
Haynes Edwin, farmer, Cross farm
Haynes Hubert, farmer
Haynes George, dairy farmer
Hickman William, shoeing smith
Jennings Wm. Jas. beer ret.Marston ferry
Marston Working Men's Club
Matthews William, Three Horse Shoes P.H
Nutt Harry Joseph, tailor, Bishop's farm
Oxford Firewood Co
Pugh Hubert William John, schoolmaster
Smith Richard, wheelwright & beer retailer
Ward Edwin, jobbing gardener
Ward Herbert, jobbing gardener
Ward Richard Joseph, shopkeeper, post office

New Marston.

PRIVATE RESIDENTS.

Allum John Frederick, William street
Akers Harold John, Main road
Akers Joseph, Main road
Austin William, Main road
Bolton George James, William street
Bray Edward L. William street
Carter Harold, Ferry road
Carter Mark, Ferry road
Clark William, Main road
Clewley John, Gordon cottages
Collett George, Tower View cottages
Cox Charles C. The Cottage, Ferry road
Daniells William John, Gordon cottages
Eaton William, Tower View cottages
Faulkner William 40 William street
Foster Mrs. Diamond villa
Giles Walter William, Main road
Gundey Edward, Main road
Gooling Frank, Main road
Gray John, William street
Green George, William street
Harris Frederick, William street
Harris William, Somerset villa
Hoster Charles, William street
Hopkins George, St. George's terrace
Lauder Frederick S. William street
Love John, Main road
Morris Frederick, Main road
Nutt Harry, William street
Pearce Frank Alfred, 47 William street
Pether Thomas White, Main road
Plumridge Harry, William street
Richardson Richard, Woodville, Ferry rd
Rogers Joseph, Carnation cottage
Shrimpton Mrs. 45 William street
Smith William, Ferry road
Street William Henry, 44 William street
Taylor Alfred, Ashmole house
Taylor Frederick, Ferry road
Thurland Henry O. Sunnyside
Webster Mrs. Lily house
West William Oliver, Main road

COMMERCIAL.

Akers William, hay binder, Ferry road
Austin Thomas, builder
Benning Mrs. laundress
Carter Mark, brick maker & farmer
Carter Louisa (Mrs.) grocer, & post office
Collis Joseph, carpenter
Cross Joseph (Mrs.) baker & dairy
Harris Jesse, police constable, William rd
Evans George, The Somerset House P.H
Goulden P. Frank, carpntr.St.George's ter
Kelsey Brothers, nurserymen, Main road
St. Clements & District Allotments Association (W. Bullock, sec)
Saunders Jas. wheelwright & blacksmith
Scarrott Shadrach, general dealer
Weller Frederick, coal dealer
West Mrs. laundress

An extract from Kellys Directory, 1913–14. (With permission from Reed Information Service)

Around Old Marston

Oxford Road, Church Lane and Elsfield Road

Aerial view of Marston village 1918.

Rose Bank, on Oxford Road, seen here c1910, when occupied by the Roberts family. Left to right: Bessie Roberts, Ann Cheal (nee Roberts), William Roberts, Dick Cheal. The property stands end-on to the road and now incorporates extensive alterations and additions.

The Roberts family c1898. Left to right back row standing: Elsie Roberts (married Jack Knapp), Florence Roberts (remained unmarried), Mary Roberts (married Richard Ward), Ann Roberts (married Dick Cheal). Middle row: Emily Roberts (married Ted Cox), Elizabeth Roberts, née Carter, William Roberts, Olive Roberts (married Jack Griffin). Seated in front: Bessie Roberts (married Albert Griffin), Margaret Roberts (died 1906 aged 20).

Oxford Road

On the opposite side of the road stands the Red Lion public house, kept by Charles Cotmore in 1895, with Bishops Farm, an early 18th century building, in the middle distance, now 41 Oxford Road.

Oxford Road looking north towards Boults Lane.

An early view down Boults Lane, opposite the Red Lion. *The Village Green by Mrs Lambourne's house was at the bottom of the village, being much smaller than it used to be. Meetings used to take place here on Sundays, Church and Chapel services were held.* Women's Institute Notebook

Halford House, 8 Boults Lane, originally a mid- to late-17th century farmhouse of limestone rubble.

Boults Lane

Boults Lodge, an early 19th century house at the bottom of Boults Lane.

An early photograph of Oxford Road with Boults Lane junction behind the grassy bank to the left. The Red Lion can be seen end-on at the right hand side, with Primrose Cottage beyond. The first building in Boults Lane, centre in the photograph, was at one time a motor cycle repair shop. The cottage on the extreme left is now demolished.

Wentworth, 38 Oxford Road, beside the Red Lion. Probably 18th century or earlier. Could originally have been pair of cottages or a single cottage with attached barn. The roof is partly thatched. The building is shown here from an old print by de la Motte 1837. Courtesy of Bodleian Library.

1930s looking north along Oxford Road.

24 Oxford Road. During the 1930s, a fire destroyed half the roof, back to the chimney. Now renovated from the chimney stack back, being half thatch and half slate.

The Orchard

The Orchard, 20 Oxford Road. The narrow way behind the wall was called The Terrace and numbers 22 and 24 Oxford Road can be seen. *The only shop in the village was kept by Mrs Drewitt, and later by her daughter, Mrs Walton, along the passage known as The Terrace. The premises were badly damaged by fire and a new bungalow was built by Mr R Wyatt for Mrs Walton on the ground opposite Court Place, with a hut at the side as the shop. This, however, was pulled down during the war.* Women's Institute Notebook.

In 1665 an Anthony Gardiner paid tax on a property, which may have been The Orchard. This was inherited in 1725 by James Gardiner, by which time it consisted of a dwelling, garden and orchard. The property was owned by John Sayer, a butler of Balliol College, and inherited by his heirs James Langford and then Ann Langford who, in 1813, sold the property to William Loder. On his death in 1818 his widow, Mary, sold the property to Richard Rippington, who married Mary Simms, daughter of James Simms, a Marston farmer who, in 1843, owned The Manor House and Cromwell House. Richard Rippington died in 1841 and The Orchard passed to his widow Mary who, in 1865, left it to their daughter Mary Cannon, wife of William Cannon, another local farmer. She in turn left it in 1876 to her daughter Mary Sims Honour who had married John Honour, also of a Marston family.

John Honour with his first wife, Mary Simms Honour, who died 1906. John Honour was a great character, a huge bearded man, and a fine builder and carpenter. He carried out the restoration of St Nicholas Church in 1883, under the guidance of H G W Drinkwater, the Oxford architect. Soon afterwards he restored and added to The Orchard; Victorian church tiles in the hall, and a woodblock floor, handmade from old church timbers remind us of his work in the church. About this time the house was called Honour's Orchard or The Orchard. The Orchard ceased to be a farm in the late 19th century, but still contains remnants of the many fine Blenheim Orange apple trees and apricots which used to flourish here. John Honour died in 1917.

Mrs Selina Honour, née Curtis, (on the right) second wife to John Honour, seen in the garden of The Orchard with Rose Gibson c1920s.

Where Orchard Cottage at 18 Oxford Road now stands was the farm yard with pond and cow sheds, all manner of sawpits, pumps, and wells behind. This area was converted by John Honour into his Builder's Yard and workshop soon after 1876. Mr Arthur Bleay seen here c1923 with Messenger's Traction Engine cutting wood. Messenger occupied John Honour's yard behind The Orchard.

Court Place, 33 Oxford Road.

Possibly early 16th century farmhouse, enlarged during the 17th or early 18th century and remodelled c1880. *The farm was owned by Brasenose College from c1500 to 1956. At one time the house was moated, being filled in c1860s. The house was originally roofed in Stonesfield slate, the last of these being removed in May 1948. There are documents in Brasenose College dating from 1361 and many of the fifteenth century, most of these documents relating to Courts Baron held at Court Place. During the Wars of the Roses, there are statements relating to important documents being signed at The Court Place.* Women's Institute Notebook.

Bishops Farm, 41 Oxford Road. An early 18th century farmhouse now house. The whole was restored in 1980, receiving an award from the Oxford Preservation Trust.

This photograph of Oxford Road c1945 shows Tom Ward delivering milk around the village. The Three Horseshoes is on the right, with the sign of The White Hart just seen, and Fir Tree House on the left, with the Reading Room hidden behind the trees. The Three Horseshoes dates from the mid- to late-18th century, and was kept in 1895 by Ronald Gurden.

Oxford Road looking south c1945, with The Three Horseshoes on the left and The White Hart tucked behind. Note the shop and post office in the middle distance, kept at one time by Richard Ward.

This photograph of 1959 is of The Yews, 10 Oxford Road, demolished early 1960. On the left is No 12 Oxford Road, known as The Hazels, formerly two cottages.

The White Hart public house on Oxford Road, a mid- to late-17th century building, seen here in the 1930s.

Looking north, the wall of The Orchard on the left hand side, the Marston Post Office on the right, with the British Legion Hall tucked in behind. The prominent white building was known as Latimer Cottage, kept at one time by Mr Eadle. The White Hart and The Three Horseshoes can be seen in the middle distance.

Richard Ward was another postmaster at Marston during the early 20th century, who also took pride in helping to keep the churchyard tidy.

Fir Tree House, 14 Oxford Road, a thatched building, originally two cottages. This was the former home of Professor and Mrs Vincent Harlow. Professor Harlow was governor of Marston Secondary School, which was renamed Harlow School. Mrs Harlow gave the church the gallery in memory of her husband.

Fir Tree House looking north, with Cross Farm barn and farmhouse and the Manor House on the extreme right.

Cross Farmhouse, Oxford Road, an early 17th century farmhouse, photographed before 1912. *Originally with thatched roof and dormer windows, the roof was replaced with old red brick tiles several hundred years ago; the bad lattice panes of the dormers were removed about 1900 by Richard Smith, the local builder and landlord of the Red Lion. Two small windows were uncovered about 1930 almost intact, the one above the front staircase revealed some old plaster work. Adjoining the farmhouse is an old tithe barn, originally thatched but re-roofed about 1920.* Women's Institute Notebook.

Cross Farm

'Boysey' Haynes outside the door of Cross Farmhouse. Her mother was known as Granny Webster.

Cross Farm is on the left. *The farm was owned at the end of the 18th century by Thomas Rowney of Oxford, passing to his son, followed for about a century by a family named Phillott before passing to the Rippington family in the 19th century who farmed it until 1885 when it was tenanted from them by Richard Haynes, passing to his son Edwin Haynes two years later. He continued to farm it and eventually bought it from the Rippington family in 1920, when it passed to his son Raymond Haynes.* Women's Institute Notebook.

Marston was renowned for its majestic trees until disease caused many of them to be felled: compare this view with the previous one. Cross Farm looking north towards the Manor House at the end of the village. The village stocks stood outside the large barn on the extreme left. The edge of the building on the right-hand side is Almonds Farm.

Demolition of Cross Farm barn in 1964.

Cross Farm workers c1940s: Hughie Harris on is on the left, Raymond Haynes second right.

The Marston Cross, from which the farm took its name, used to stand a little way from the house to the north east, in what is now the garden of Cross Cottage. This view is of c1826. *'There are no remains of antiquity in this place except two rude stone crosses, one of which is in the church-yard, the other in the street, without either carving or inscription on either and both mutilated.' Gentleman's Magazine,* 1800

Church Cottage at 7 Elsfield Road, pre-1964, with Cross Farm in right-hand background: *all that survives of a group of cottages close to the church wall. Two cottages in the churchyard facing the school were pulled down to enlarge the churchyard. These were occupied by Mr Vials and Mr Fathers. It was also extended on the north side, a pond being filled in, and the wall built round. Church Cottage used to be a line of three cottages; one of these had a gateway leading into the churchyard, the windows also looked that way.* Women's Institute Notebook

A view from the church tower across Elsfield Road. The barn of Almonds Farm occupies the site of what is now numbers 2 and 4 Elsfield Road. Church Cottage in the foreground.

Elsfield Road

Cross Cottage on the left and Church Cottage on the right, viewed from the junction of Oxford and Elsfield Road. Cross Cottage has now been extended and the gateway is no longer there.

The junction of Oxford Road on the right with Elsfield Road on the left is still called The Cross, or Cross Corner. The building is Almonds Farmhouse, No. 1 Oxford Road.

4 Elsfield Road, originally part of Almonds Farm. Converted into a residence and large garage by Lord Howard Florey in the 1960s. Lord Florey, Professor of Pathology at Oxford from 1935 died in 1968. His second wife, Margaret, also made a career in science and collaborated with her husband in research. During 1939 to 1941 work by Florey, Ernst Chain and colleagues, including Margaret Jennings (later Florey), showed that penicillin, discovered by Alexander Fleming in 1928, but neglected for ten years, was a true chemotherapeutic agent. Florey, Chain and Fleming shared the 1945 Nobel Prize for Physiology and Medicine. Margaret Florey died November 1994.

The Old Vicarage in Elsfield Road, known as Norcott, seen here in the centre. *The first vicar to live at Marston was the Reverend Smith, in a newly built house, now the present Vicarage. Where the Vicarage now stands were three cottages occupied by Bray the butcher, Jakeman the wheelwright, and Mrs Ward.* Women's Institute Notebook.

Church Farm

Church Farm, an early 18th century farmhouse, possibly earlier. A three-unit plan with evidence of a through passage, later altered into an L-shape. This is one of the traditional family farms in the village, belonging to the Loder and Haynes families in the 18th and 19th centuries.

At Church Farm Robert Loder the second placed a stone, with R.L. 1818, over the door ... His son, also Robert, was a pork butcher and bacon curer and used an underground tank for curing ... the chimney for smoking was pulled down years ago by Mr Drewitt. Robert Loder the third had a large family but most of them died very young in the 1850s.

Mr Harold Haynes, son of Mrs Flos Haynes, at Church Farm. The garage was on the site of a Bacon Factory Curing Tank. This photograph was taken 1974; the site is now new housing. *Mr Luin, a butcher of Church Farm, was noted for making sausages, pork and meat pies, and curing of hams and bacon. He employed a number of men.* Women's Institute Notebook

May morning 1974. Mrs Flos Haynes of Church Farm and the Morris Dancers of Headington. Mrs Haynes was the daughter of William Kimber of Headington Quarry, famous for his Morris Dance music. The dancers 'danced' Mrs Haynes from Church Farm to the Bricklayers Arms. Mrs Haynes died 1980.

Ponds Lane, behind the church, in 1968. Aptly named after the ponds which used to surround the church and the streams which used to run along the roadsides.

Oak Lodge, east of the church in Church Lane, apparently of 18th century origins.

The Bricklayers at the end of Church Lane, seen here probably pre-1960.

Outing from the Bricklayers c 1940s.

Behind the Bricklayers were the allotments known as 'The Butts', which were used at one time by the university as a rifle range. Joseph Henry Bleay is seen here in c1940s.

Mill Lane Area

The Manor, Cromwell House and Alan Court

Cromwell House, 17 Mill Lane.

A Manor House of the early to mid-17th century, possibly partly earlier. This photograph is pre-1912, at which time the building was extended and work included the moving of dormer windows from the back to the front of the building. Probably built c1622, and known as Cromwell Castle during the 19th century.

The Civil War and the Croke family

Just before the Civil War, in 1637, Marston again became a separate parish. In 1617 Unton Croke, the lawyer and son of the legal family of Croke of Studley Priory, married Anne Hore, heiress to a house and land in Marston. This house was on the site of Cromwell House and Manor House and is shown on the Langdon map of 1605. It was rebuilt by Unton Croke after their marriage, probably about 1622, but some materials from the older house, such as doorways, beams and panelling, can still be seen. The house was known as the Mansion House in the Headington Manor Court Rolls until the mid-nineteenth century; the present names came later, after the division and virtual rebuilding of the property by the Sims family.

Unton Croke bought more land as he progressed in the legal profession, and he became a leading Parliamentarian in the Civil War (1642 to 1646). So it is not surprising that when, in 1645, Charles I with his court and forces were besieged in the city of Oxford, General Thomas Fairfax maintained his headquarters for a time in Unton Croke's house and was visited there by Oliver Cromwell. The surrender of the city was signed in this house in May 1646. The following month, William Bell, Minister of the Gospel, preached in Marston church to *Sir Thomas Fairfax and the General Officers of the Army, with divers other officers, souldiers and people*. One can picture the activity in Marston during those four years: troops and horses billeted in the farms and cottages, requisitioning of crops and livestock, felling of timber, and much wear and tear on houses and roads. The roads were green tracks also used for pasturing animals, and bordered by streams and ponds which were still clearly shown on the 1876 Ordnance Survey map, and have only disappeared in living memory. Top soil was removed from the fields to the west to make earth-works, and a temporary bridge built over the Cherwell.

In 1670 Unton Croke died. His elder son Richard became recorder of Oxford and lived at Marston, probably at Cross Farm, until 1683, and he was succeeded by his son, Wright Croke. Their handsome memorial is in the chancel of the church. The house was inherited by a great niece, Anne Yorke (née Bishop), and some of the land, together with Cross Farm, was bought by Thomas Rowney the elder. Both he and his son, Thomas, were attorneys in Oxford and Members of Parliament.

The Manor and Cromwell House

Cromwell House and The Manor House, 15 and 17 Mill Lane during the 1950s.

The occupants of Cromwell House c1898, at the rear of the house. Left to right back row: George Green, George Henry Mathews, Mildred Gurden, William Henry Mathews. Front row: Annie Green (née Mathews) with baby Violet, Nelia Mathews (née Gurden), grandson William Mathews known as Chick.

Cromwell House, with the Manor House. Mill Lane sweeps round to the left, leading to the Ferry; Ponds Lane on the right. Cromwell House was occupied by Mr G N Clark, (later Sir George Clark) in the 1930s until his appointment as Provost of Oriel College.

Manor House, 15 Mill Lane, early 19th century, partly earlier. May incorporate part of the Manor house noted as having been built by Unton Croke and used as Fairfax's headquarters during the siege of Oxford in 1645. Originally one building with Cromwell House but divided c1840. It would seem that the approach to the Manor House was changed at the time of the rebuilding of number 15, and this may explain the handsome gatepiers standing some twenty yards north of the houses, now seemingly stranded in private gardens. Occupied during the 1930s and 40s by Mr and Mrs Arthur Henry Vernéde. Mr Vernéde was elected as a parish councillor from 1928.

Alan Court

Alan Court, formerly Home Farm, viewed from across Mill Lane c1965.

Home Farm, Mill Lane c1905. Rebuilt in the 1930s by Shotto Douglas and an archway and large iron gates added at the south end. Occupied by Mr Wood in the 1940s and by Peter Nye in the 1960s, and afterward by Dr Peter and Dr Elinor Williams. The family in this photograph would appear to be that of Frank Haynes, the little boy is Bernard Haynes born 1899. Bernard was later a well known organist in the church.

Albert Edward Bleay, who died in 1935 aged 73. This photograph was taken c1920. He lived at 11 Mill Lane and was a gardener and rose grower, with an allotment on 'The Butts'.

Taken from the church tower, a rear view of Alan Court with 1930 timbered addition and Old Barn. The Manor House can be seen with farm buildings behind, together with the roof and dormers of Cromwell House.

William Ward, on left with brother Wally Ward, on the Ward dairy horse and cart in Mill Lane.

Herbert Ward, more often known as 'Uncle', was responsible for most of the thatching in the area.

The Haynes family in 1937 at 60 Mill Lane. Left to right: Betty Haynes, Tom Haynes, Tom Haynes snr, Mary Ann Haynes, Joyce Haynes.

Mary Ann Haynes celebrated her 100th birthday on 5 March 1987. She was the village's first centenarian, and was given VIP treatment at her home in Bradlands council flats, where the South Oxfordshire District Council organised a party for her.

Brasenose Cottages, just north of Cross Farm, in Mill Lane. These were the most photographed buildings in Old Marston. Frequently referred to as The Old Cottage, or Pond Cottage. This view was taken before 1912.

The wall of Cross Farm can just be seen here on the left-hand side. Note the three children sitting on the grass to the right. During the 1930s the building was often called Granny Cotmore's cottage. Mr Webb, the carrier, called daily on his way to Beckley. A large 'W' was hung on the outside of the cottage if the carrier was required to stop and collect. *Most of the older people wore smocks, the children wearing theirs with a black belt. They seldom left the village, the shopping being done by carrier. A packman which came on horse-back, pedlars with cottons, buttons, ribbons, laces and books, also a tinker with pots and pans, who did the mending of same.* Women's Institute Notebook

The Old Cottage, showing
the line of the wall to the
side of the pond.

Demolition of The Old Cottage, February 1940. Left to right: Dick Ward (of the post
office), Billy Ward, Dick Payne, ?.

The Ferry

A ferry has crossed the Cherwell at Marston since the 13th century. At that time the freehold was held by two fishermen of Oxford, but the exact position of the crossing is not known. The ferry is not shown on a map until 1876 and at that time consisted of a line stretched across the river and a punt-type boat pulled across by hand. A public house was established next to the Cherwell, originally The Ferry, now known as The Victoria Arms. It was reached via a path from Mill Lane, known as Green Way. A backwater close to The Ferry was called Marston Lake.

This view of the Victoria Arms across the Cherwell shows the Ferry in relation to the river bank. The river has always been popular with members of the University for punting, and the Victoria Arms was a popular place to stop for refreshment.

This photograph of the early 1900s shows the family of Biovois, who, at that time owned the Ferry Inn and ran the Ferry. It was Victor Biovois who renamed The Ferry Inn the Victoria Arms, after Queen Victoria. In front Emma Biovois née Bustin (1858–1935), Victor Celestin Biovois (1862–1936). Middle row: Hannah Theresa Biovois (1884–1941) married Herbert Edward Ward, Ernest Victor Biovois (1886–1916 from wounds received in France) and Adele Constance Fanny Biovois (1890–1963). Standing at back is Percy John Celestin Biovois (1887 died ?1964) *The ferry was known as Frenchman's Ferry. The family was Biovois, but was generally spoken of as 'Boovoys' or something of that sort.* Memories of 1910.

Victor Biovois aboard the ferry. In 1915 Kellys Directory shows his occupation as that of carpenter, living at Fern Cottage.

A beautiful snow scene across the Ferry. *The deep snow in January 1881 completely isolated the village, tunnels were dug up the main street. A man named John Irons died. My father came to Oxford in a trap to do the business for the Family, was gone all day. He could not get back by road as it was blocked by Copse Road, known then as Crossground Corner, could only get back by crossing the field, snow-drifts were twenty feet deep in places and the snow laid on the ground for weeks.* Women's Institute Notebook

Another snow scene, dated 1908. Note the snow covered plants to the right of the building, shaped and hollowed so that a person could sit within them. These bothies, as they are called, were more generally known as 'the Boffies'.

By 1879 the road itself, which begins at Banbury Road in North Oxford, was a private road called Northern Meadows after the farm of that name. It became Marston Ferry Road at the beginning of the 20th century but was then only a short length ending at No 15 and the Oxford City and County Bowls Club.

Evidence suggests that a temporary bridge over the river was erected across the Cherwell from Marston meadows c1646 by Thomas Fairfax, the parliamentary commander during the Civil War.

Marston Ferry Road.

The only links between Marston and North Oxford was the ferry: until the opening of the extended Marston Ferry Road on 12 November 1971. *Five school children today cut the tape to open the £616,000 Marston Ferry link road in Oxford - 44 years after it was first planned. The five children were (left to right) Michael Ray, 13, of Harlow School; Deborah Lee, 10 of St Nicholas School; Owen Kyffin, 10 of St Aloysius School; Caroline Kay, 10 of Oxford High School for Girls and Xante Mellor, 17 of The Cherwell School, watched by Ald. Miss Ann Spokes. They were chosen from the five schools along the ¼ mile route to stress the road safety benefits of the road. After the ceremony the official party, including the Lord Mayor of Oxford, Ald Tom Meadows and the chairman of Oxfordshire County Council, Ald. Viscountess Parker, drove along the new road before it was opened to the public at noon.* Oxford Mail 12 November 1971.

School and Recreation

St Nicholas Church School, from Elsfield Road.

The church school of St Nicholas was built in 1851 on glebe land, owned by the church. An early headmaster was Jesse Rothwell who, with his wife, is buried in the churchyard next to the school. During World War II Marston was home to evacuee children. Local children would attend school in the morning and the evacuee children in the afternoon. The school catered for children up to the age of 11, thereafter children were taken to Gosford Hill school in Kidlington. The old school closed in July 1954, after 103 years' service, and is now used as the village hall. A new school, St Nicholas County Primary, was opened September 1954.

The school 1954 taken from the church tower. The house opposite is No 10 Elsfield Road, Cannons Farm.

An early school group of 1913.

An early photograph of Elsfield Road. The children are possibly going to a church service.

'Scholars of Marston School, making their own playground', as reported in *Jacksons Oxford Illustrated*, 20 April 1927

The school prided itself on its garden, situated on land opposite the church, now occupied by bungalows. The school master on the right hand side may be Mr Chapman. He lived in the Almonds at No 1 Oxford Road, then moved to a bungalow behind the Memorial Ground opposite the White Hart. *The Village Pound, now the site of 6 Elsfield Road, stood opposite the school, an enclosed place where cattle were kept and a sum of money had to be paid to claim them back.* Women's Institute Notebook

Left to right, back row: — Robinson, — Holt (?), Winnie Tomlinson, ?, — Webb. Middle two: — Drewitt, — Ayris. In front, kneeling: ?, ?, Queenie Ayris, — Reynolds. The occasion was a Vicarage Garden Party, and this group of dancers, c1910, performed Maid of the Mountains.

May Day played an important part in village and school life. Children during the 1940s parade down Mill Street and into Alan Court.

Alan Court played host to this annual event, which attracted a large audience.

Each year girls were chosen as May Queen and her attendants and officially 'crowned'. The Reverend John Mortimer can be seen in this photograph.

Schoolchildren gathered to watch the ceremony.

Parents and visitors enjoying the sunshine and the dancing.

Prizes were also awarded for the best May Garland, sometimes prepared with mother's help. Taken c1954, from left to right: Katherine Bleay, Leonard Maund, Dorothy Edwards, Janet Saunders.

The older children, too, took part in this competition. Left to right: ?, ?, Eileen Fowler, John Bleay, Hazel Ward.

This dance troupe is performing in Boults Lane, c1940s.

The British Legion Hall with the Marston Post Office next door in 1964. The Hall, sometimes referred to as The Workman's Hall, was originally a mission hall believed to have been established by Congregationalists in 1871, and built by John Honour of The Orchard, and was used for many years by the British Legion and the Women's Institute. Reproduced with permission from Alun Jones

'Aunt Sally' was a popular pub game at The White Hart, as at many Oxfordshire pubs. This photograph was taken in the 1940s.

Members of The British Legion, seen here in 1937 for the coronation of George VI, includes Curly Slaymaker, Tom Haines, Bill Edward, Cliff Colley, Bill Lambourn, Wally Jenkins and Bert Ward.

A later photograph taken for the Coronation Review 1953. Left to right, seated: Snowy White, Tom Haines, Fred Chaulk, Bill Osbourne, Jim Mott. Middle row: Les Clarke, ?, ?, Ernie Keller, Joe Gratten, Arthur Simpson, ?, Harry Bridges, Arthur Gregory, George Morris. Back row: Bill Faulkner, ?, Fred Overton, ?.

An early outing, possibly of members of The Women's Institute.

It was in the upper, or Reading Room as it was called, that the newly formed WI held its first meeting in 1922 and where it continued to meet for the next seven years. The War Years brought change. By this time the Institute had moved across the road to the British Legion Hall and what had previously been their home became the overflow for the Village School. When the Legion Hall obtained a licence in 1948 the Institute moved back to the Reading Room. They were now the tenants of the Church to which Mr Mortimer had given the building.

Mrs E M Chaundy joined the Women's Institute in 1921 and is seen here in 1965, aged 84. Mrs Chaundy, together with other pensioners, formed a band called The Crackpots, and played old-time music at various clubs in the district. Mrs Chaundy was leader of the Marston Good Companions, a club for the elderly.

1971 the demolition of The Workman's Hall, opposite The Orchard, the former mission hall, and home to The British Legion. The site became what is now Hayles Stores.

The Reading Room

After the death of Mr John Honour of The Orchard in 1917 the building used as his workroom was first rented and then sold by Mrs Honour to the then Vicar, the Reverend J H Mortimer, who converted it into a Reading and Club Room for the men of the village; but it was not long before it was being used for all the village activities. The upper, or Reading Room as it was called, housed the village meetings and the lower rooms were used by the school for cooking and other class activities.

The Marston Market was held to raise funds for the church restoration, c1959. Left to right: Mrs Dorothy Carter, Mrs Agnes Kensington, Mr Hugh Kensington, Miss Sally Harley, Mrs Lindsay Harley, Mr Eva Savage, Mrs Barnsley, the Reverend Gordon Savage.

The back of the Reading Room on the right, Orchard Cottage on the left. Showing Mrs Mona Davies, with Ruby, Jonathan Heatley, Tamsin Heatley in the pram, c1959.

The Reading Room housed the Youth Club during the 1950s. This group c1956 includes Christine Carpenter, Delia Hickman, Monica Case, Geoff Carter, Brian Carpenter, parish worker Miss Lylles, Brenda Saunders, Ruby Baker, Tony Carpenter, Lorna Widdows, Sylvia Clarke, Joyce Baker, Sandra Frost and Tony Higgs.

1959 Demolition of the Reading Room, with Tom Haynes.

With the passage of time the Reading Room fell into disrepair and it was felt that the structure was not sound enough to justify any large amount being spent on repairs.... At last the time came when the children moved to the new Primary School and the Reading Room was no longer considered safe for large gatherings. It was at this point that a member of the Church offered to buy the Reading Room on condition that the purchase money should be used to convert the old Village School into a much needed Church Hall. The land on which the Reading Room had stood would then be given back to the Church to be converted into a Memorial Garden in memory of the late J H Mortimer who had, during his long incumbency, done so much for the village. This, however, left the Church with the not inconsiderable cost of demolition. But Marston has never lacked benefactors and another member of the congregation offered to bear this cost. It was only left for a Committee of local gardening experts to be formed and a subscription list opened and the money was forthcoming for outlay and maintenance. Women's Institute Notebook

New Marston

The 1876 Ordnance Survey Map of New Marston shows hardly any building in the area. There was a row of some eight cottages called Tileworth Cottages on the Main Road, which had formerly been called Marston Lane, and later was to change to Marston Road. These cottages were occupied by labourers from the brickworks and clay pits in the area behind. William Street was laid out but not named and the map shows one dwelling on the north side. Part of Ferry Road was laid out but not named, and ran from the Marston Road to the lane which still runs into Edgeway Road. Beyond that no road is indicated. Edgeway Road seems to have been a tree-lined lane and was originally called Hedgeway Road. Beyond this area to Marston village there was nothing but fields. One field, opposite the Church on the other side of the Marston Road, was laid out as the Oxford University Athletic Running Ground and there was a pavilion on the north west side of the oblong track.

On the map of 1900 we see that William Street, Ferry Road and Edgeway Road are all named and that development has taken place in the form of sporadic building, in groups of two or three houses, along the three roads and on the Marston Road, but the northern limit to this is still the south side of Edgeway Road, apart from Tileworth Cottages. The Mission Hall is named.

A number of house fronts still bear dates, from which we can follow the development: 1877 on the front of 30 William Street, *South View Cottage* March 1888 (49 William Street), *Portway House* April 1889 (51 William Street), *Tower View Cottage* 1890 (228 Marston Road), *St George's Cottage* 1891 (234 Marston Road). By 1911 the population of the whole of Marston was still only slightly more than seven hundred people.

The main period of building in New Marston took place between 1934 and 1938, and the Municipal Housing Scheme covered new roads to the west of Marston Road. (Extracts based on a booklet prepared in 1978 to celebrate the 50th anniversary of St Michael's Church of England First School, New Marston.)

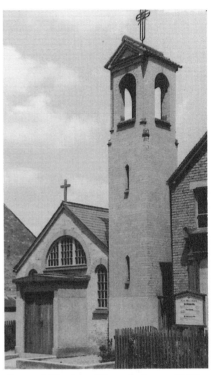

Mission Church (Ferry Road), erected by Mr Bray, September 1911 at total cost of £252 12s 0d.

In 1888 the Reverend Charles Morris of Marston and the Reverend Edmund F G Tyndale of Headington, among others, were instrumental in securing a site for a new church to accommodate the population of the District of New Marston, which, at that time, was about 400. The cost of the site and the new building was estimated at £900. The Mission Room was originally built to become two cottages, but, being considered unsafe, was used as a Mission Church from 1889 to 1911, when the church was built in Ferry Road, being a daughter chapel of St Nicholas Church at Marston. The Mission Room then had a varied career, being at one time an old furniture shop. It was bought back in 1936 by the vicar, and on occasions, has had services held in it, but otherwise is used as a clergy-and-choir vestry. (January 1942)

Interior of St Nicholas Church at New Marston c1930 before alterations.

The Church re-opened in April 1937 after extensions, the cost of which was £355. The East Window and Reredos is in memory of Ada Louisa Jackson (Mrs C Nugent Jackson). The Dedication Service also included the Blessing of the New Chancel, the Children's Corner, the Dedication of the adjacent Mission Room, the tower and bell, and the pulpit and Altar rails.

Church leaders Easter 1929, taken outside St Nicholas chapel of ease in Ferry Road. The Reverend Howard-Rose is at the centre. The chapel served the community of New Marston until the formation of a new parish, St Michael and All Angel. The Chapel building is now a tyre depot.

A Children's Service, Easter 1929.

Outside Ferry Road church c1936. Back row: Ted Lowe, Mr Akers, Arthur Lowe. Seated: Mr Gallop, ?, Harry Elmey, Mr Morris.

Mothers Union group of c1942.

St Nicholas New Marston, St Dunstan's Carol League party Christmas 1930, taken outside New Marston post office on the corner of William Street and Main Road (now Marston Road). Left to right: Bubbles Hind, Marg Gurden, Reg Harris, Winnie Evans, Vic Johnson, ?, Joyce Hansford, ?, Micky Walker (with lamp), John Lowe, – Howse, Bernard Brown, Bill Rhymes, Vic Rhymes, Norman Brown, ?, ?, Margaret Palmer, – Lowe (front centre), ?, ?, ?, ?, Harry Smith (with song sheet), ?, Harold Walters (boy with flat cap), Lucy Martin, Una Carter (girl in white coat), Hilda Clifford, Hugh Howard-Rose, Rev Howard-Rose, Doris Akers, ?, ?.

Sunday School outing c1930s. Left to right back row: Margaret Palmer, Ethel Belson, Winnie Evans, ?, ?, Rev Howard-Rose, ?, ?, ?, – Hawes, Lucy Martin, Mabel Clifford. Middle row: ?, ?, Ethel Gurden, Gertrude Faulkner, ? (behind), Bubbles Hind, ? (behind), Evelyn Belson, Kathy Smith (behind), Mary Deacon, Doris Akers (behind), Lorna Evans, ? (behind), ?, ?, ?, Josephine Hawes, Phyllis Webster, Joyce Hansford, Iris Clifford (behind), Phyllis Webb, Jimmy Giles. Front row: Alfie Cross, Vic Rhymes, ?, Norman Brown, ?, George Webster, ?, ?, – Smith, ?, Sidney Webb.

The Audrey Shave Junior Dance Troupe c1943, believed to include Elizabeth Gilkes, Marion Edwards, Sylvia Dobbing and Diana Goodchild. This dance troupe used to practise in the church hall.

The Audrey Shave Senior Dance Troupe c1943, believed to include, left to right back row: Audrey Shave herself (back row 1st left), ?, Dorothy Reason, Florrie Cooper, Eileen Petty, Dorothy Phipps, Sheila Hunt. Front row: June Cooper, Beryl Madden, Valerie Elmey, ?, – Holt, Jeannette Claydon.

New Marston War Memorial

The memorial is on the east side of Marston Road, opposite the playing fields of Trinity College and Lady Margaret Hall, and adjacent to St Michael's School. The parish church of St Michael and All Angels at the junction of Marston Road and Jack Straw's Lane is about half a mile away and was not built until 1954-56.

The memorial, about nine feet in height, stands on a stepped plinth and has a red-paved surround. It consists of a pillar, on top of which are four small pointed arched surmounted by a cross. The main face of the pillar faces the road and has twenty six names from the 1914-18 War with rank and regiment:

Pte A G Akers 2nd OBLI	Cpl A Harley R Berks
Pte H Akers R1 West Kents	1st Cl Stoker C Hartwell RNR
L/Cpl H Allum 2nd 4th OBLI	Pte L Heath 1st? 4th OBLI
QrM Sergt H Baker 1st OBLI	Pte T Madden 1st OBLI
L/Cpl F C Burborough 5th OBLI	Pte R Matthews 10th Bn KSLI
Pte J R Cross QOOH	Cpl F Newport RFA
L/Cpl G T Cummings 1st 4th OBLI	Pte C Phipps OBLI
Pte T C Dearlove 1st 4th OBLI	Bodr W Plumridge RFA
Pte P J Evans 8th Glos Regt	Sergt M Shrimpton QOOH
Rifleman R Faulkner 2nd Bn KRRC	2nd Cl Seaman W Shrimpton USN
Pte E Gough RAMC	Pte P ? Smith R Berks
L/Cpl F Gray 5th OBLI	Pte C Tolley 1st 4th OBLI
Pte T Green Rl Fusls	Pte J Walton 1st 4th OBLI

The 'nine o'clock' face has the words:

In Grateful
Remembrance
of the Men
From this Village
who laid down
their Lives in The
Great War(s) 1914–1919
and 1939–1945.

The 's' of 'wars', and mention of the Second World War are clearly later additions to the memorial, as are the names of a further eleven men.

Tom Bailey	Frederick Matthews
James Crank	George Thomas
Walter F Giles	Norman Wakeley
Gordon Hert	Dennis Ward
Ernest MacKenzie	George Wiggin
Kenneth Young	

Postcard of New Marston early part of this century, looking north. The two houses on the left are still standing, the third property became the site of a garage and now stands derelict, the fourth property, with handsome bands of brick, was demolished to make way for the car park of The Somerset House.

The Somerset House public house on the junction of Marston Road with Ferry Road. Seen here in 1968.

Coronation Street party, 1953, at The Somerset House on Marston Road.

Left to right, back row: Queenie Hamilton, Lillian Austin, Iris Evans, Mrs Green, Alice Flint, Martin Flint, Alice Giddins, Mrs Booker, Olive Evans (landlady), Connie Claydon, Mrs Claydon, Mrs Pearce, Mrs Townsend, Mrs Jerrett, Mrs Mackenzie, Margaret Young, Mrs Harris, Thelma West, Paul West. 2nd row: Mrs Kendrick, Ruth Evans, Lil Austin, Susan Beyer, John Madden, Iris Madden, June Claydon, David Claydon, Kathleen Pearce, David Green, Peter Batts, Janet Austin, Judy Kendrick, Kathleen Baughan, John Kempson, Rodney Beauchamp, Colin Harris, Margaret Mackenzie, ?, ?, Valerie Booker, Mrs Booker, Rosemary Webb, Ruth Mackenzie, Mrs Walters. 3rd row: Jonathon Evans, Richard Fenton, Anthony Pearce, Christine Cupples, Ivor Newport, Barrie Fenton, John Mackenzie, Anne Pearce, Brian Cupples, Laurence Waters, Janet Flint, Kay Giddins, Alan Bruce, Nigel Waters, David Young, Alison Kendrick, Lister Evans, Carol Evans, Eileen Young, David Norridge, Trevor Norridge, Colin Townsend, ?, Sheila Townsend, Jonathon West, John Washbrook, Jasmin Booker, Audrey Harris, Colin Harris, Eliza Madden. Front row: Brian Young, Mrs North, Jenny North, Anthony North, Christine Beyer, Stephen Beyer, Carol Madden, Rosemary Baughan, ?, ?, Jack Evans (landlord), Christine Evans, Robert Turley, Ann Turley.

An extract from Kellys Directory, 1932.
(With permission from Reed Information Service)

EDGEWAY ROAD (New Marston), from Main road.

SOUTH SIDE.

1A, Simms Leonard
1 Simmonds Fredk
2 Finch Mrs
2 Jones Geo.Fredk.carpntr
   Weller Fred, road transport contrctr. (The Garage)
3 Young Harold
4 Gray Alfd
5 Waine Harry
6 Madden Jn
7 Couling Fredk. Jas

JUBILEE COTTAGES :

1 Meads Wm
2 Fletcher Jas
3 Beesley Mrs
4 Parrott Hy
5 Scarrott Mrs. Rose, genl. dlr

   Tolley Mrs. (Roselea)
King Harry V.(Ford cott)
Gurden Rd
Walton Jas
Beesley Benj
Young Jsph
20 Ward Percy
21 Tunstall Edwd
   Inwood Archie (Arrlen)
   Izzard Mrs. (Everleigh)
23 Greenwood Geo. cycle repr
24 Adams Hy. Thos
25 Tolley Wm
26 Cooper Ernest Thos
27 State Wm
   Hounslow Mrs
   Howson Herbt. (Southerley)
   Claydon Albt. (Berlice)
   Avery Regnld. (Elnathan)

NORTH SIDE.

Brown Wm. (New Bungalow)

EDITH ROAD (Grandpont), from 112 Abingdon road to Chilswell road.

NORTH SIDE.

2 Aldridge Mrs
4 Jago Ernest Alfd

18 Bates Miss
18 Southorn Harold
19 Beauchamp ErnestChas
20 Cox Frederick George
21 Cox George
22 Phipps Percvl. Wltr
23 Clarke Mrs. E. J
24 Denniss Mrs
24 Bint Frank, sign writer
25 Rolfe Arth. Fras
26 Bolton Lewis

WILLIAM STREET (Headington), from 35 South street to 15 Church st.

NORTH SIDE.

1 Morris Arth. Wm. Thos
3 Acaster Wm. Alex
5 Grain Mrs.Ada,beer retlr
7 Currill Wm

SOUTH SIDE.

2 Rimmer Mrs
2A. Cobb Alfd
4 Ovenden Wm
6 Ovenden Mrs
8 Jeffs Arth
9 Fleetwood Thos. Hy
10 Bazeley Chas
12 Allworth Mrs
14 Goodgame Rt
16 Keen Fredk. Chas
18 Smith Fredk

WILLIAM STREET (New Marston), from 12 Main road.

NORTH SIDE.

1 Akers Albt
3 Phipps Mrs
5 Hern Chas. Thos
7 Palmer Chas
9 Webster Mrs
   Janaway Wltr. P. (The Nest)
19 Hurley Chas
21 Dearlove Hilbery
23 Lee Frank Regnld
25 Dearlove Wm. Edwin, insur. agt
27 Martin Mrs
29 Salvage Wm. Hy
31 Hawes Edwin Chas
33 Stockford Geo. Herbt
35 Cross Mrs. Eliz
37 Hausford Wm
39 Bolton Mrs

41 Webster Michl. Geo
43 Knight Chas. Hy
45 Rhymes Stephen
47 Deacon Hy. Arth
49 Harris Regnld
51 Ward Herbt. Edwd
53 Harris Wm
55 Norman Wm.Edwd.Geo
57 Benning Mrs
59 Webster Thos
61 Webster Albt. Thos
63 Faulkner Thos
65 Hind Geo
67 Vallis Stephen Wm

SOUTH SIDE.

   Boys Scouts (Oxford Group) (headquarters)
2 Bossom Jsph. Jas
4 Allum Jn. Fredk
6 Kethro Miss
8 Giles Alfd. cycle agt
10 Matthews Thos
12 Harris Geo
14 Hawkins Rt. Chas
16 Lambourn Cyril Arth
18 Nutt Mrs. Florence
20 Fruin Wilfred Jn.assist. insur. supt
22 Green Geo
24 Harris Fredk
26 Cooper Bertie
28 Johnson Josiah
30 Harris Geo
32 Hall Jn. Albt
34 Rogers Fredk
34A. Dandridge Harry
36 Thurland Mrs
38 Benning Geo
44 Street Wm. Hy
46 Shrimpton Jn
48 Smith Sergt.-Maj. Jn. T. masseur
50 Wicks Fras. Hy
56 Marlow Leeson
58 Evans Jn
60 Clifford Regnld. Michl
62 Webster Fredk. Wm
64 Messenger Chas. Hy
66 Paterson Jas
68 Belson Chas. Edwin
70 Bowell Wm. Edwin

   Williams lane.
Now included in GODSTOW ROAD

Area map of Old and New Marston, 1922.

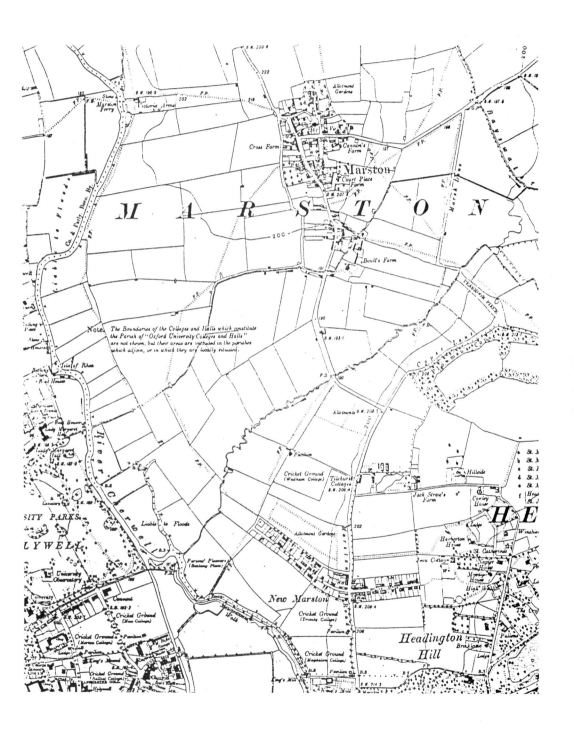

View of William Street from Main Road (Marston Road) c1900.

William Street c1907. The middle building is reputedly the oldest building in the road.

Mr Stephen Rhymes, c1921, with four of his seven children at 45 William Street. Left to right: Lucy, William, Stephen, Victor, Albert (known as Son).

Mr and Mrs S Rhymes in the garden of 45 William Street. The high wall in the background is part of the laundry built on the rear of number 49, one of the cottage industries built to serve the needs of the University. Mr Rhymes worked as a chauffeur and gardener.

Outside number 45 William Street. The tall laburnum tree was a feature of the Street for over thirty years, before its removal in the early 1960s. Left to right: Rita (née Poulter), Stanley, Peter and Lucy Rhymes.

Home on leave during World War II, Albert Rhymes (RAF), Victor Rhymes (Oxon & Bucks Light Infantry) with their father, Stephen Rhymes. The open view in the background is from William Street, looking towards Harberton Mead, at this time allotments, now the site of Prichard, Peacock and Moody Roads.

Lucy Rhymes with her youngest son, Peter, at work on their allotment, now the site of Moody, Peacock and Prichard Roads. The row of horsechestnut trees marks the line of Harberton Mead. Mrs Rhymes was never to be seen without an apron or pinafore and described as 'always at work', raising her family of seven children and two of her grandchildren.

VE Day Party, 1945, in the Scout Hall in William Street.

1 Barbara Hudson, 2 Bert Rodaway, 3 Joan Rodaway, 4 Mrs Bossom, 5 Deane Rodaway, 6 Rose Hudson, 7 Mrs Humphreys, 8 Cyril Hudson, 12 Sheila Knight, 13 Miss Bossom, 14 Mrs C Weller, 17 Mrs Stockford, 18 Harold Wiggins, 19 Mrs Wiggins, 23 Ken Bossom, 24 Peter Rhymes, 25 Jonathan West, 26 Christopher Perry, 27 Mrs West, 30 Bruce Pearce, 32 Pamela Bossom, 33 Pat Weller, 34 Molly Weller, 35 Mr Perry, 36 Mrs Perry, 37 Mr Goodall, 38 Mrs Goodall, 39 Mr Fred Weller, 40 Mrs Weller, 41 Michael Phipps, 42 Mrs Phipps, 43 Mrs Kerval?, 44 Barbara Kerval?, 46 Peter Kerval, 47 Bet Weller, 51 Andrew Moran, 52 Martin Moran, 53 Peter Stevens, 55 Christine Pool, 56 Janet Humphreys, 57 Maureen Phipps, 58 Brenda Moran, 59 Pat Townsend, 60 Mr Cox, 63 Iris Goodall, 64 Janet Townsend.

The snow house built in the road under the street lamp indicates there were no problems with cars in William Street back in the winter of 1946. The gas light outside number 50 was one of many requiring to be manually lit at dusk every night.

Daphne Cottage, No 29 Ferry Road, c1910, home to the Carter family at this time. Mrs Maria Carter and her youngest daughter Enid at the door.

Titcombe family of Ferry Road c1907. Left to right back row: Edith, Mary (known as 'Pop'), Rose. Middle row: Edward, Frank Titcombe, Lizzie, Mary Titcombe née Weller, Elizabeth called Kate, Frank. Front row: Flo, Bill. Edward Titcombe, seen in picture in scout uniform (note the hat on the ground), later married Emily Hunt from Osney and several years later lived in Kings Mill at Marston, leased from Magdalen College.

Mary Titcombe with her brothers and sisters on her 70th birthday party: Aunt Lis Madden née Weller (later known as Granny Madden of Marston), Jim Weller, Mary Titcombe née Weller, Fred Weller. Taken c1934.

At Mary Titcombe's 70th birthday party c1934, the Weller grandchildren. Left to right, back row: Gwendoline Titcombe, Georgina Cummins, baby Hazel, Granny Mary Titcombe, baby Anne, Eileen —, Frankie Bird. Middle row: Joan Smith, Florrie Cooper, Sylvia Bird (behind), Maurice Titcombe, Frankie Titcombe, Norman Titcombe. Front row: June Cooper, Graham Dobson, John Dobson, Billy Mitchell.

The Weller family outside No 1 Edgeway Road c1928 on the occasion of the confirmation of daughter Mary (Molly). Fred ran the family coal business advertised by the plaque on the house, from a yard at the back of the terrace of houses, known as Hazel Terrace. The business was started by his father, James, c1890, when the family moved from Jericho Gardens. Mrs Weller's family, the Fletchers, lived in Jubilee Cottages, a short distance down Edgeway Road, known as Hedge Way Road in the late nineteen century. The sign on the house reads 'Weller & Son, Coal, Coke, Wood Dealer. Carting done, honest possible price'. Left to right back row standing: Rose, Fred, George, Jim. Seated: Joan, Mr Fred Weller, Bet, Mrs Beatrice Weller with Pat, Molly. Alec sitting in front.

The Brickworks

The Carter family c1898. Left to right: Una, Mark Carter, John, Albert, Maria Carter. Enid in the front. Taken at the back of 29 Ferry Road.

Sale Catalogue of 1911 'The Brickfield is situate on the slope of the hill, at the foot of which runs the Public Road, and it is therefore convenient for carriage and for draining the workings and for bringing the ground into use again after the clay has been exhausted. The clay is of good quality and produces a brick of even colour, and the quantity is sufficient to last many years. The pit from which the clay is dug is situate at the rear of the works and at a convenient distance from it is placed the Drying Sheds and Kiln capable of burning 42,000 bricks. The Brickyard being situate in a district where building operations are in full swing and new estates in course of development, there is likely to be a constant and increasing demand for the bricks. 3.75 acres let to Mark Carter for many years past.'

Tileworth Cottages, on the Main Road (Marston Road), were used by workers of the brickworks. Seen here from the 1911 Sale Catalogue where they are said to be 'all let to good Tenants at Rentals of 2/6d per week each, and they each contain 2 Living Rooms and 2 Bedrooms over, and joint use of w.c., there being four for the eight dwellings. The City water is laid on to them.'

Tileworth Cottages on the right looking north along the Marston Road. The cottages eventually became derelict, and are believed to have been used during the war for fire precaution practises. They were demolished in the late 1940s.

Jackstraws Farm

Jackstraws Farm, detailed in the 1911 Sale Catalogue, included a *useful cart and Waggon Shed with open lean-to on the West side and a range of four roomy Pigstyes on the East side with enclosed Hovel at end. Brick-built Stable with iron roof. Large timberbuilt Barn on brick base with tiled roof. Extensive brick-built and slated T-shaped Granary approached by a flight of stone steps on East side and a range of very useful open Sheds under used for various purposes. At the South end of same is a man's Room with fireplace and brick floor and a Stable adjoining with timber-built and slated Granary over fitted with corn bins. On the East side of the buildings is an enclosed Cow Yard with open Cow Shed with standing room for eight cows. Two good Stables under granary, four useful brick and slated Pigstyes, brick-built and tiled boiler houses with feeding room adjoining. The apportioned rent for this Lot will be £85 per annum.* At this time the farm buildings were let to Mr Mark Carter.

The farm yard at Jackstraws Farm.

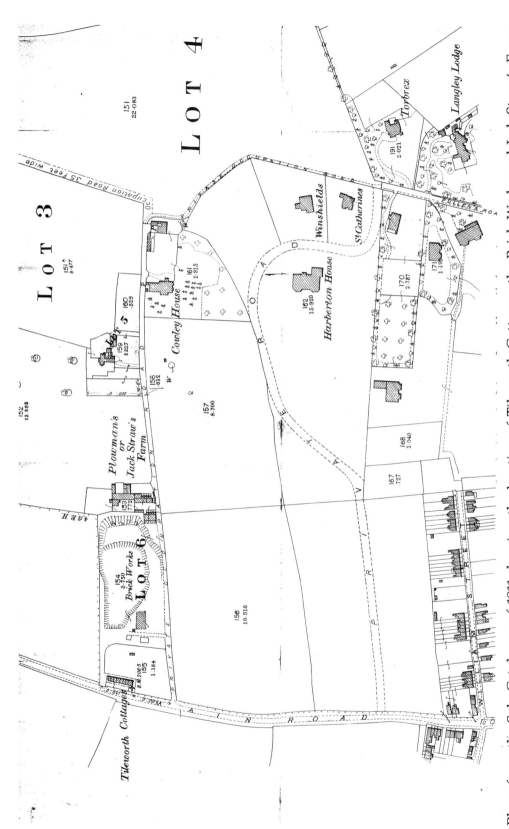

Plans from the Sale Catalogue of 1911 showing the location of Tileworth Cottages, the Brick Works and Jack Straw's Farm. Note that Marston Road is called Main Road at this time.

New Marston School

The National School near the Church in Marston village was the closest school north of St Clements, up to 1927. The school became overcrowded and younger children were sent to St Clements. To ease this situation a temporary school was started in New Marston in the Scouts Hall on the corner of William Street, which had been built about 1913 by Miss Peto in memory of her brother.

Evelyn Chandler was headmistress when the school opened in 1927. Seen here at the back of the scout hall, left to right back row: Alfie Cross, Bob Rawlins, Vic Rhymes, Harold Walters, Syd Webb, ?. 5th row: ?, Dan Young, ?, Ray Gunning, Fred Webster, Reg Greenwood, Arthur Howes. 4rd row: Ken West, Lionel Lee, Gertrude Young, Florence Giles, – Howse, Cathy Smith, Miss Chandler, Alice Howse, Eva Rawlings, Pat Weller, ?, Bill Rhymes. 3rd row: ?, ?, Joyce Hansford, ?, ?, Mary Gurden, Bet Weller, ?, Harry Smith, Bob Rogers. 2nd row: ?, Mary Deacon, Eileen Harris, Bubbles Hind, Jean Webster, Betty Smith, Rita Giles, Linda Gray, Jimmy Giles. Front row: Frank Smith, Nora Smith, – Phipps, ?, Phyl Stevens, Ethel Gurden, ?, Doris Walton, ?, Billy Claydon.

The class of Miss Blanche Beatrice Simms c1927. Left to right, back row: Bill Rhymes, Dan Young, ?, Ray Gunning, Fred Webster, Reg Greenwood, Arthur Howse. 3rd row: Nora Smith, ?, ?, Phyl Stevens, Miss Simms, Doris Walton, Mary Gurden, Lorna Evans, ?. 2nd row: ?, Mary Deacon, ?, Bubbles Hind, — Webster, Betty Smith, Rita Giles, Linda Grey. Front row: Ken West, Billy Claydon, Lionel Lee, Frank Smith, Bob Rogers.

Bishop Shaw dedicating the Church of England School at New Marston 24 May 1928. Land for the school was donated by Mrs G Herbert Morrell from her estate centring on Headington Hill Hall in 1927 and the school was built by May 1928, opening ceremony on Thursday 24 May. Money had been raised by local subscription, and the sum of £1,700 was raised in just over six months. Mrs Morrell declared the building open, and was presented with bouquets of flowers by two of the scholars, Josephine Hawes and Robert Rawlins. The Oxford Times also advises us that '*The local troops of Girl Guides, Scouts and Cubs were on parade, the former being under the charge of Miss Hobson and the latter under Serjt-Major Smith'.* The official name of the school was New Marston, Oxfordshire, Church of England, Junior, Mixed and Infants.

Group of children outside the new school building c1930.

The school opened on 10 January 1927 and Miss Evelyn C Chandler was appointed Head Mistress, assisted by Miss Blanche Beatrice Simms. There were 46 children transferred from Marston village, aged between five and ten. By September there were 63 children. On reaching the age of 11, the children returned to the top class in Old Marston and this continued for a short time until New Marston school was opened.

The whole school seen here c1938.

On 10 September 1930 Miss Ruth Carter was appointed to take charge of the 40 Infants, aided by Miss Lucy Hutchins. Miss Carter became Head of Infants and retired from the school in July 1968. By December 1930 the school had 102 pupils on the roll. Once more the Scouts Hall was in use for the younger children.

April 1935 there were 36 infants in the Scouts Hall and school was still awaiting extension, three classrooms finally opened on 29 February 1936. These opened out into 'one large hall', and the area is now converted to the school hall. By 1938 another extension: 2 new classrooms, opened on 12 November 1938 - these being the 2 classrooms beyond the hall. On 12 November 1938 283 children on the roll.

25 September 1939 double shift arrangement started today, owing to the evacuation of school children from West Ham, London. New Marston children attended school from 8.30 to 12.30 this morning. Star Lane school West Ham will be using the building from 12.45 to 4.45. (Star Lane moved to four halls in the area by May 1941 and school resumed full-time schooling.)

19 September 1945 Victory Party is being held in the School after the afternoon session.

22 December 1947 resignation of Miss Chandler and Miss Simms. 1948 new Head Teacher, Mr John Headley Thomas Jones and 'Miss Mabel Carter began duties as a qualified Assistant in the Infants Department' and 'Mrs Daisy Gurden began as Domestic Assistant, and to help at school during dinner hour'. 11 January 1949 301 children on roll. The New Marston County Primary School in Copse Lane was completed in the spring. In May, 17 children were transferred there. The school was officially opened 4 November. By 20 December the two schools had defined 'catchment areas' bordering on Headley Way. Extracts from School Booklet prepared in 1978 to celebrate 50th anniversary.

During 1937 the Marston Road was widened. This view shows the Somerset House on the left, William Street on the right, looking north.

Again during 1937, with the junction of Jack Straws Lane on the right. The name of this road dates from at least 1932, although the road was not officially adopted until 1954. The name of Jack Straw used to be common. It is possible that Jack Straw, a priest and participant in the Peasants' Revolt of 1381, stayed at a farmhouse here; or it may be commemorating Jack Straw, a wealthy and respected gentleman who farmed nearby in Headington.

Kings Mill on the River Cherwell, the southern boundary of Marston, seen here late 18th century at a time when it appears derelict. There had been a mill on this site for many years. Painting by William Turner of Oxford, reproduced here with kind permission from the Ashmolean Museum, Oxford

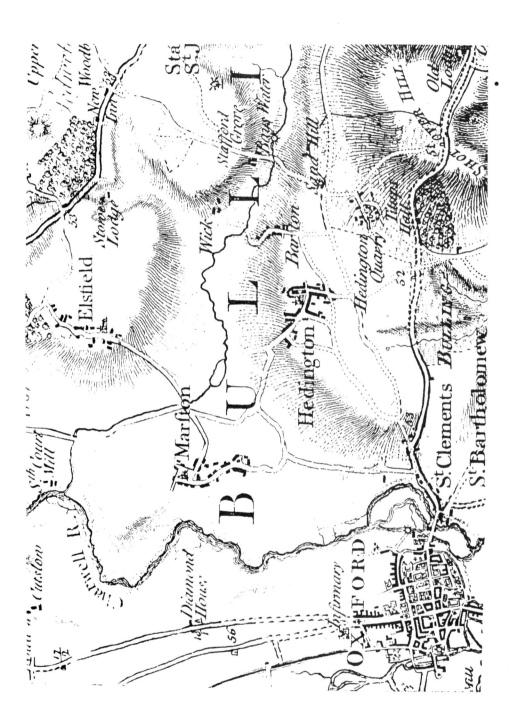

The Kings Mill can be identified on this map of 1769, by Jefferies, being what appears to be the only building on the present day Marston Road.